Judith Blacklock's Flower recipes for
WINTER

The Flower Press

Published by
The Flower Press Ltd
3 East Avenue
Bournemouth
BH3 7BW

A CIP catalogue record for this book is available from the British Library.

ISBN 13: 978 0 9552391 1 3

Design: Amanda Hawkes

Printed and bound in China by C & C Offset Printing Co., Ltd.

Contents

Introduction

Colour, fragrance and sparkle can fill your home during the cold winter months. Good design does not have to be complicated or expensive and my aim has been to provide a book that shows how good flower design is accessible to all.

This book contains over 40 ideas using easy to obtain flowers and foliage. To create each design I give simple, logical steps using my many years experience as a teacher and designer. I want it to be easy for you to create a beautiful home that has the warmth that can only be achieved with the welcome of fresh flowers.

Follow these designs faithfully if you wish. However if you do not have walnuts in your home think of substituting small fir cones. If yellow roses are half the price of red roses consider using these instead perhaps adding chilli peppers and berries to bring in a touch of red. Just follow the overall shape of the design using plant material of the same form – round, line or spray – and it will be difficult to go wrong. Any design can be made festive with baubles, glitter and tinsel that we all hoard until this time of year.

Many people think that gardens are bereft of flowers during the colder months but think of holly and skimmia with their wonderful red berries, the luscious black berried fruits of the ivy, fir cones of all sizes and the wide variety of evergreen foliage.

As for flowers, I rarely cut them from the garden whatever the time of year. I love to see them growing and to extend the home outdoors. The florist can provide a whole rainbow of colours.

The time is right for amaryllis, gerberas and roses in rich jewel colours, early bulb flowers and pot plants such as poinsettia and cyclamen.

You only need a few techniques to complete the designs found in this book and they are all explained in the easy to follow section at the back. There is also a colour index of some of the flowers and foliage that are available during the winter months and a glossary of the equipment that you will need to get going and where to get it.

Enjoy your flowers

Judith

Apricot ripple

You will need

- tall glass container
- smaller, inner container of the same form
- stones or pebbles
- salal (*Gaultheria*)
- flat roses – I have used David Austin roses but you could use the last of the garden roses which often flower until the end of the year
- dried poppy seedheads
- beads and decorative wire (optional)
- dried *Hydrangea* heads
- gold spray paint

Design tip

The pebbles accentuate the colour of the roses, but you could substitute the pebbles with cloves, shells or fruits.

This design uses glorious fragrant roses. The addition of dried poppy seedheads and hydrangea, lightly gilded, gives a seasonal flavour.

Method

1 Place the smaller container in the centre of the glass vase and fill the cavity between the two containers with stones or small pebbles.

2 Wedge floral foam in the opening of the small container. Alternatively, place a small dish on top of the inner container that is lower than the rim of the outer container. Place foam so that it rises above the rim.

3 Spray a dusting of gold spray paint over the *Gaultheria* leaves and create a structure of leaves (Techniques page 97). Your objective is to create a mass of leaves and flowers that is about one and a half times the volume of the visible container.

4 Add your roses.

5 Thread a bead onto a length of decorative wire and twine this around the tip of a poppy seedhead. Repeat and add to the design. If you do not have decorative wire just add gilded poppy seedheads.

6 Add the gilded *Hydrangea* to fill in any gaps and give a full luxurious feel to the design.

Classically exotic

You will need

- natural textured container
- blue spruce (*Abies nobilis*)
- small *Aspidistra* leaves
- *Eucalyptus* pods
- berried ivy (*Hedera arborescens*)
- fir cones
- 1 stem white *Cymbidium* orchids
- silver baubles

Design tips

If the stems on your orchid heads are not long enough then place them in tubes before adding them to the design.

The *Aspidistra* leaves give smooth texture that contrasts well with the spruce. If *Aspidistra* leaves are unavailable use more berried ivy instead.

A traditional arrangement with a contemporary twist, this design has a base of blue spruce, *Eucalyptus* pods, rolled *Aspidistra* leaves and wired fir cones, accentuated with stunning white *Cymbidium* orchids.

Method

1 Create a strong outline of foliage using the spruce (Techniques page 93).

2 Manipulate the *Aspidistra* leaves (Techniques page 97) and place them throughout the design, along with the other foliage and *Eucalyptus* pods. Wire the cones (Techniques page 95) and position to give contrast of texture.

3 Place the orchids in groups to complete the design.

Winter firelight

This impressive mantelpiece decoration will warm any room. Early tulips in moss covered containers, candles in apples (the centre removed with an apple corer) and fir cones are linked with trails of honesty seedpods.

You will need

- 3-4 small rectangular containers or glass tumblers
- adhesive tape
- moss
- 9-12 tulips
- 4-5 red apples
- 4-5 tapered candles
- fir cones
- honesty (*Lunaria*) seedpods
- reel wire or raffia

Design tip

You could use feathers rather than honesty and oranges or tangerines covered in cloves as an alternative to apples.

Method

1 Make a grid over the top of each container using the adhesive tape.

2 Place 2-3 tulips in each container.

3 Cover the containers in moss, concealing the sides and the tape at the top. Secure the moss with wire or raffia.

4 Use an apple corer or sharp knife to create a hollow in the apples that will fit the candles snugly. Try not to go through to the other side of the apple.

5 Arrange the tulips and the candles on the mantelpiece with some fir cones. Thread the honesty pods on gold decorative wire and add to the arrangement.

Festive fountain

This fun contemporary design uses a fountain of bear grass to create space and movement.

You will need

- **gold container**
- **1 bunch of bear grass (*Xerophyllum tenax*)**
- **decorative reel wire**
- **floral foam**
- **small beads with holes big enough to allow them to be threaded onto the bear grass**
- **14-16 roses**
- **angel hair**

Take care

Be careful when handling bear grass. If you slide your hand down the stem you may get a paper cut.

Method

1 Secure the bunch of bear grass together at two points with the decorative reel wire – about 2.5 cm (1 in) from the bottom, and at the point from which you would like it to 'fountain'. This will determine the height of the design.

2 Place the soaked foam into the container so that it rises above the rim, and push the bunch of bear grass firmly into the centre.

3 Thread beads onto the bear grass.

4 Cut the roses short and insert them into the foam around the base of the fountain. Angle them so that they form a rounded mass.

5 Add a little angel hair over the roses for sparkle.

Lily blooms

This design captures the beautiful delicacy of white *Lilium longiflorum* blooms by contrasting them with dark, fragrant pine bound with decorative wire.

You will need

- a variety of large and small glass containers
- opaque cellophane
- lengths of pine (*Pinus*)
- decorative reel wire
- 3-4 stems of white *Lilium longiflorum*
- white ribbon
- pearl pins

Design tip

You could use this technique to create a matching mantelpiece arrangement, or a garland to adorn a staircase. If you find it difficult to obtain decorative reel wire the pine will also look good unbound. At the end of the festivities throw the pine on an open fire and its fragrance will fill the room.

Method

1 Line some of the smaller containers with cellophane.

2 Bind the pine with the wire to create a linear form. You will need one stem per container.

3 For the smaller vases, bind the pine into a circular wreath and place on the rim of the vase.

4 Remove the lilies with long secondary stems from the main stem to fill the larger containers compactly. Bind them together with the ribbon and secure with a pearl headed pin.

5 Place a few lily heads in each of the smaller vases.

All in a row

You will need

- several identical coloured glass containers
- mini *Gerbera* for each container
- green *Trachelium*
- bunches of small baubles in a co-ordinating colour

Design tip

You could use another mini flower instead of a *Gerbera* such as a rose or a carnation, but make sure it has a strong round form.

This delightful row of containers uses coloured glass and matching gerberas to make a bold statement. As you can see they could also be placed in a circle for a different effect.

Method

1 Half fill the containers with water.
2 Cut your flowers short and place them with the baubles and *Trachelium* in different combinations in the containers.

At the double

You will need

- **2 containers of the same shape and of the same material – ideally one should be smaller than the other**
- **floral foam**
- **florists' tape**
- **cocktail sticks**
- **mixed foliage**
- **2 stems spray chrysanthemum**
- **ornamental twiggy balls**
- **1 stem Chinese lanterns (Physalis alkekengi var. franchetii)**

A tall, striking design ideal for the buffet table.

Method

1 Wedge soaked floral foam into the two containers so that the foam rises about 5 cm (2 in) above the rim of each container.

2 Place several cocktail sticks, at regular intervals, onto a length of florists' tape and attach round the base of the smaller container. Impale the sticks into the foam of the larger container.

3 Create a domed outline with the foliage in the two containers so that most of the foam is covered.

4 Cut the ornamental twiggy balls short and add to the design.

5 Cut the stems of Chinese lanterns into shorter lengths and place in the foam. Wire the orange slices (Techniques page 96). Insert these in the foam.

6 Add the individual heads of the spray chrysanthemums.

You could use fir cones
sprayed silver instead of
the twiggy balls.

Winter welcome

You will need

- wire wreath frame or a coat-hanger bent into a circle – a 30 cm (12 in) frame will create a ring of a suitable size for most front doors
- wreath moss
- garden twine or strong reel wire
- 2-3 branches of blue spruce or a bundle of berried ivy
- fruit, ribbon and baubles to decorate

Winter wreaths are lovely as door hangings. Alternatively they can be used in the middle of a table, perhaps with a candle in the centre.

Method

1 The base

- Tease out the moss, removing any stones or twigs.

- Make the moss into around 15 tight balls, each about the size of an orange.

- Attach the end of your wire, or twine, to the top of the frame.

- Place the first moss ball on the frame where you have attached your wire.

- Wrap the wire tightly around the frame and the moss 2 or 3 times to secure – leaving about 2.5 cm (1 in) between each wrap. Continue until the frame is evenly covered, but do not cut the wire.

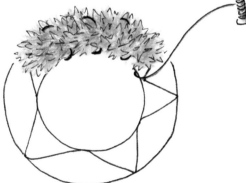

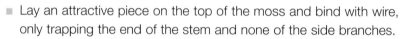

Design tip

Instead of spruce you could use any combination of mixed evergreen foliage such as ivy (*Hedera*), *Skimmia* or yew (*Taxus*). Leaves take in water through their surface as well as their stem ends so immerse the foliage in water for 30-60 minutes before using so that it is well conditioned.

2 The foliage cover

Using spruce (see design on the previous page)

- Take a branch of spruce and cut it into smaller pieces. Each piece should be no longer than 12 cm (5 in).

- Lay an attractive piece on the top of the moss and bind with wire, only trapping the end of the stem and none of the side branches.

- Place less special lengths around the inner and outer edges and bind in with wire to create a thick, three-dimensional effect. Work around the circle slowly, overlapping each previous placement by about 70 percent so that you get a thick, luxurious ring.

- Before cutting the wire make a loop for hanging.

Using berried ivy (see design on the right)

- Cut your stems of ivy into approximately 12 cm (5 in) lengths. Bundle 2 or 3 together. Continue as if using spruce.

3 To decorate

- Attach baubles, fruit, flowers in orchid tubes and ribbon as desired (Techniques page 95).

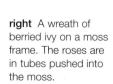

right A wreath of berried ivy on a moss frame. The roses are in tubes pushed into the moss.

Cranberry compote

A mass of mouthwatering cranberries in an unusual silver birch container.

You will need

- container made of natural material such as bark
- floral foam
- flat moss
- cranberries
- angel hair

Design tip

To create a similar container, stretch a thick rubber band around a plastic container. Place strips of bark or coconut fibre under the rubber band all round the container. Hide the band with sisal or ribbon (see the diagram on the right).

Method

1 Place the foam into the container so that it rises to just below the rim. There is no need to soak the foam.

2 Make a bed of flat moss on top of the foam.

3 Spread the cranberries evenly on top of the moss.

4 Tease out the angel hair to make a fine, flat layer, and place this over the entire design.

Ivy connection

You will need

- 2 identical tall vases
- 2 ivy trails
- 2 flowers – this design uses a rose and a *Freesia* but you could use any two flowers of your choice.
- Christmas baubles
- fir cones

Design tip

You could substitute virtually any flower for the two used, but it is important that they are in scale. Each flower should be no more than twice the size of the other. Try and reflect the colour of the flowers in the colour of the baubles.

Method

1   Fill the two vases with water and link them with the ivy trails.

2   Place the rose in one vase and the *Freesia* in the other. Make sure that the two vases appear balanced.

3   Place the baubles and fir cones around the base each vase in a pleasing formation.

Rich and mellow

You will need

- **copper container**
- **7-9 artificial fruit picks in warm tones (Glossary page 107)**
- **7 red roses (here I have used *Rosa* 'Grand Prix')**
- **7 orchid tubes**

Design tip

If you were using a brass container you could use yellow and gold flowers to bring out the tones of the metal. For silver and tin containers try using greys, blues and pinks. Terracotta is a good alternative to copper.

The rich copper tones of this container are accentuated by the warm rich fruits and deep red roses.

Method

1 Arrange the fruit picks in the container making sure that they rise high enough above the rim to create good balance. If they are not long enough you may need to put a small amount of foam in the bottom of the container to add height. The foam would also make the picks more secure.

2 Insert the roses into water filled orchid tubes.

3 Place the roses throughout the design.

Pepperpot

A quick and easy design that is perfect for a contemporary home.

You will need

- a square container made of coloured Perspex or glass – this one is 15 cm (6 in) square
- floral foam
- coloured sisal
- metallic black pepper berries (*Schinus molle*)
- 9 yellow roses

Design tip

Black laurestinus berries (*Viburnum tinus*) would look good in place of the pepper berries, or use *Skimmia* or *Hypericum* berries for contrast.

Method

1 Cut the foam so that it fits the container with a 2.5 cm (1 in) gap on each side.

2 Fill this gap with the sisal, pushing it down with a knife, so that the foam is completely hidden.

3 Add the pepper berries around the edge of the design so that they cascade over the edge of the container.

4 Cut the roses short and insert them into the foam so that they are in neat rows. Add more berries if there are any gaps.

Woodland lights

You will need

- rectangular wooden container, lined with a tray or black bin liner
- floral foam
- 3 square candles
- 2 stems of myrtle (*Myrtus*), box (*Buxus*) or other small leaved foliage
- 3 stems of red spray St. John's wort (*Hypericum*)
- 3 stems of ming fern (*Asparagus umbellatus*)
- 10-12 small roses
- baubles in a complementary shade

Design tip

If you do not have ming fern just use more of your small leaved foliage to cover your foam but ensure that it hangs over the rim of the container.

This delightful arrangement uses a container made of bark to create a country atmosphere. When using candles in a design at Christmas add baubles to reflect the light and create sparkle.

Method

1 Make sure that your container is waterproof. Line with a black bin liner if there is any chance of leakage.

2 Place a piece of soaked foam into the container, making sure there is room around the edges to add more water. The foam should be just lower than the rim of the container.

3 Position the three candles along the centre of the foam. Add tape and sticks if unstable (Techniques page 94).

4 Add the flowers, foliage and baubles around the edge of the design. You may wish to group the roses as shown, or spread them more evenly. Keep the stems short so you do not overwhelm the container.

Rose topiary

You will need

- **glass container, approximately 30 cm (12 in) tall**
- **floral foam**
- **20 roses, around 60 cm (24 in) in length**
- **rubber band or florists' tape**
- **5-7 *Aspidistra* leaves**
- **ivy trails (*Hedera*)**
- **rose hips, *Skimmia*, or other berries**
- **salal (*Gaultheria*)**

Design tip

You can easily create this design in a ceramic pot and it will look just as effective.

Decorate your home with this simple yet effective 'tree' of long-stemmed roses.

Method

1 Prepare the container by lining it with one or more *Aspidistra* leaves with their stalks removed. Add a piece of foam that rises about a quarter of the height of the container above the rim.

2 Strip the roses of all their foliage and thorns.

3 Arrange approximately 15 roses in the hand with their stems parallel so that they form a gentle dome.

4 Use florists' tape or a rubber band to keep the stems together – just under their heads and towards the base. Cut the stems to the same length and insert firmly into the centre of the foam.

5 Cover the foam with your foliage and manipulated *Aspidistra* leaves (Techniques page 97).

6 Insert the remaining roses at the base in two groups. Use the berries to give additional colour and interest through the design.

7 Make sure that both ends of the ivy stems are bare of leaves. Push one end into the foam at the base. Twine around the stems to the top. Wrap round the stems firmly and twine back to the base. Insert the other end of the ivy stems into the foam.

Basket of roses

This simple design is made seasonal by the use of winter foliage and the sparkle of iridescent angel hair.

Design tip

***Elaeagnus*, *Skimmia*, berried ivy (*Hedera helix* 'Arborescens') or holly (*Ilex*) would work equally well. Evergreen foliage will last for several weeks but you may need to replace the roses after about a week.**

Method

1 First line your container with cellophane or bin liner to make sure that the basket does not leak.

2 Add soaked floral foam to just below the rim of the container. Cut off any excess cellophane.

3 Create an outline with the *Osmanthus*, radiating the stems from the centre of the container (Techniques page 93).

4 Place your roses evenly throughout the design.

5 Drape a little angel hair over the top of the roses.

"Not Brussels Sprouts!"

This is one to cause comment. Easy to create and dual purpose as the sprouts can be cooked afterwards if you remove their supports carefully.

You will need

- floral foam
- small container for the flowers
- cocktail sticks
- Brussels sprouts
- assortment of seasonal flowers and foliage – I have used anemones and *Skimmia* berries

Design tip

Anemones love water – if the frilly greenery around the neck starts to look wilted submerge the flower under water to revive. Keep the water topped up. For a party you can make this container several days in advance. It should be wrapped in Clingfilm® and kept in the vegetable drawer in the fridge.

Method

1 Cut a piece of foam into a vertical column that is sufficiently wide and tall to hold your container. Do not wet the foam. The design shown uses foam measuring 10 cm (4 in) x 10 cm (4 in) x 15 cm (6 in) high. The container is 5 cm (2 in) across. The design can be scaled up or down.

2 Press the container firmly into the foam. Do not insert too much pressure or the foam will split. Remove container and with a knife cut out the piece of foam so that your container will fit. The rim of the container should rise just above the foam.

3 Cut the cocktail sticks in two. Trim the sprouts so that they have a smooth base. Insert a stick into the base of each sprout and position them in the foam. Repeat until the foam is covered.

4 Pour water into the inner container. Cut your plant material and add to give good proportions.

You will need

- **rectangular or square glass container**
- **glass pebbles**
- **set of under water LED lights with integral batteries**
- **5-7 white _Cymbidium_ orchid heads**

Design tip

Cymbidium orchids last well underwater. Change the water daily and the flowers will last up to a week. They are ideal for this design as their transparency makes them appear to glow.

You could also try this design with roses, anemones or fir cones.

Winter glow

An electrifying display of illumination which will cast an unusual alternative to candlelight. These amazing lights are totally safe and effective underwater.

Method

1   Make sure that the glass pebbles are completely clean before putting them in the bottom of the container.

2   Fill the container with water.

3   Turn on the lights and bury them amongst the pebbles so that the light is evenly spread.

4   Add the _Cymbidium_ heads to the design. You will find that if you do not have sufficient they will float to the surface, so add more until you get the desired effect.

Elegance

A long-lasting structure of coral fern with the addition of a few beautiful roses.

You will need

- tall container – this one is silver to harmonise with the pink roses
- glue and glitter
- 3-5 stems coral fern (*Gleichenia polypodioides*), dried
- 4-6 pink roses
- silver bullion wire
- purple beads

Design tip

The stems in a bunch of coral fern can be gently separated and manipulated so that the fronds of fern form a circle. You can use the coral fern fresh or dry in this arrangement – either way it will last a long time.

Method

1 Add a little glitter to the coral fern (Techniques page 97) and insert the fern into the vase of your choice.

2 Place the roses in the centre of the coral fern so that they create a gentle dome shape. Cut them short so that their stems are not visible above the rim of the container.

3 Make a garland of beads by threading each one individually onto the wire and twisting to hold in place. Drape the garland over the top of the coral fern.

Textured layers

This glorious candle arrangement will need no care and attention and will always look good. It uses texture, form and colour to give designer impact and not a single flower is required.

Design tip

It is important to have the smallest or lightest aggregates at the base as they would otherwise filter to the bottom. Here the heavier aggregates weigh down the lighter and maintain the layered effect.

If you wanted to add a fresh ingredient you could include a few stems of the chocolate coloured *Rosa* 'Leonidas' amongst the baubles, with their stems in orchid tubes filled with water.

Method

1 Pour the aggregates into the vase in layers so they rise just short of the rim of the container.

2 Place a shallow piece of foam to fit the neck of the container. It should not rise above the rim. There is no need to wet the foam.

3 Tape 4 or 5 cocktail sticks around the base of the candle with florists' tape or use hairpins of wire (Techniques page 94). Place the candle on top of the foam.

4 Add the wired sprigs of baubles around the rim of the container, draping them down to give good balance.

Simple and stylish

This minimalist design would look striking in any contemporary home.

You will need

- tall cylindrical vase
- thick white church candle
- florists' fix
- 2-3 stems deciduous holly (*Ilex verticillata*)
- bag of tiny shells

Design tip

You could use beans, pulses, cranberries, sand, cloves or glass beads in place of the shells.

The holly stems will last well out of water.

Florists' fix will only adhere to a clean, dry surface.

Method

1. Place a small amount of florists' fix on the base of the candle and secure it to the bottom of the vase.

2. Pour the shells around the candle. Fill about one quarter of the vase.

3. Cut the holly stems into shorter lengths and place around the candle. They should rise about two-thirds up the container.

Blue Christmas

The blue of the spruce is teamed with harmonising whites and greys with a festive spirit introduced with the shine of the Christmas baubles.

You will need

- low bowl about 25 cm (10 in) diameter and 12.5 cm (5 in) high
- floral foam
- 1 medium branch of blue spruce (*Picea pungens* 'Glauca')
- 7-9 fir cones
- 7-9 white roses
- *Eucalyptus* seed pods
- laurestinus (*Viburnum tinus*) berries
- 2 stems *Eucalyptus cineraria*
- bunches of mini baubles on wire stems

Design tip

I have used *Eucalyptus* and *Viburnum tinus* but any foliage you have would work.

Eucalyptus pods are only available at this time of year but they will last all year.

Method

1   Wet the foam and place it in the bowl so that it rises just above the rim.

2   Make a circular outline with the blue spruce cut into short lengths. Angle stems down over the rim of the container but do not overpower it with stems that are too long (Techniques page 93).

3   Wire the fir cones (Techniques page 95) and add in groups. Add the roses.

4   Place the remaining plant material, also in groups, to fill out the design, making sure that the finished proportions of plant material to container are one-and-a-half to one.

5   Choose mini baubles, in a colour to coordinate with your container, and position to give balance of texture, form and colour.

Poinsettia

You will need

- potted poinsettia (*Euphorbia pul cherrima*) plant
- container with a natural texture, such as bark, high enough to disguise the plastic pot
- length of silver ribbon
- medium gauge wire

This poinsettia needs little enhancement – a simple bark pot and silver bow set it off to perfection.

Method

1 Place the poinsettia in its pot into the container.

2 Create a bow shape at one end of the length of ribbon and bind it at its centre with wire. Make sure you leave enough wire to poke into the soil.

3 Insert the wire into the soil and wind the rest of the ribbon around the base of the plant.

Design tip

Never purchase a poinsettia that is displayed outside a shop or near the door as this plant is particuarly vulnerable to draughts and will consequently not live for long.

Light as a feather

As individual placements for the dinner guests, or arranged in a line along the centre of the table, this design is sure to attract attention.

You will need

- small container about 8 cm (3 in) high. This could be a small tumbler, terracotta pot or jam jar
- strong evergreen leaf or leaves, such as large ivy, if you are using a clear container
- small piece of foam
- handful of white feathers
- rose in colour of your choice

Design tip

This is also an ideal design for Valentine's Day – simply use red feathers and add a single red rose such as *Rosa* 'Grand Prix'.

Method

1 Cut a piece of foam that will rise about 2 cm (1 in) above the rim of the container. Soak the foam and insert in the container. If you are using a glass container wrap a long lasting leaf or leaves around the foam before placing inside.

2 If the white feathers are long economise by cutting each one into two sections. Insert the feathers out of the top and sides of the foam to give a good covering so that you do not see the foam. Angle others down over the rim but take care not to overwhelm the container. Use feathers with the cut edge lower so they are covered by those with finer tips.

3 Take the single rose and cut short at an angle. Place in the centre of the feathers.

Subtle peaches

This luxurious design uses an alternative winter colour scheme of chocolate, palest peach and black to create a sophisticated look.

You will need

- low black ceramic container – mine is 20 cm (13 in) in diameter
- floral foam
- thick candle
- blue spruce
- garden foliage such as *Pittosporum*
- coloured baubles of various sizes
- 1m (40 in) organza
- 1 medium gauge florists' wire
- 5 large peach roses or 7-9 smaller roses

Take care

If you light the candle ensure that the flame is well away from the material. *Never leave a lighted candle unattended.*

Method

1 Place the foam into the container so that it rises about 7.5 cm (3 in) above the rim. Secure the candle into the foam (Techniques page 94).

2 Use the spruce to create a strong outline (Techniques page 93).

3 Introduce one or two placements of garden foliage. Keep each type of foliage together rather than scattering it throughout the design. Take care to maintain the overall shape you have created with the spruce. I have made one group of chocolate *Pittosporum tenuifolium* 'Purpureum' which is easy to grow in the garden but difficult to find at the florist. You can substitute the foliage for any that you have available.

4 Add the baubles in one or two groups.

5 Take the length of organza. Fold one third over so that the fabric that creates the rosette is thicker and stiffer. Wind the wire around one end of the roll – this will make the other end splay out in a rosette shape. Add this to the design along with the baubles.

6 Group the roses at the front of your design to give a strong focal area.

53

Self contained

You will need

- a tall terracotta container
- a small plastic dish to fit the opening of the container
- floral foam to fit the dish
- florists' tape
- a round candle
- heavy gauge wire
- medium gauge wire
- fir cones
- wreath moss
- china grass (*Liriope muscari*)

Design tip

I used a very tall container but this design would look equally effective in a terracotta long-tom.

A stylish design using neutral tones that will harmonise with any interior.

Method

1 Place the soaked foam into the dish. Place over the opening of the tall container and secure with florists' tape. You can simply wedge the foam directly into the container if you are satisfied that it is waterproof.

2 To secure the round candle, heat a few lengths of heavy gauge wire gently over a flame and insert them into the base (Techniques page 94).

3 Wire the fir cones (Techniques page 95).

4 Cover the exposed foam with moss. Pin it in place using the wired cones, angling them upwards. Secure using hairpins made of wire.

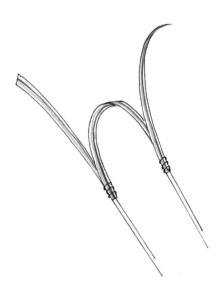

5 To make the loops of china grass, make a fold around 15 cm (6 in) from one end. Pinch together at this point and then bind and extend with wire. Repeat at the other end. Insert each wire into the foam so that loops are formed in between, to create enclosed space and rhythm.

You will need

- large low dish or plate that will hold water
- floral foam
- 3 purple ornamental cabbages (*Brassica*), ready glittered or natural
- 7 roses – I have used *Rosa* 'Avant Garde'
- 1 m (40 in) organza
- bunch of baubles on wires
- spray filler – I have used statice (*Limonium*)

Design tips

The stems of the cabbages are very thick. To make insertion easier, sharpen the ends to a blunt pencil point with a knife.

'Blue' roses are shorter lived than other roses and more susceptible to bruising, so handle with care.

Sumptuously regal

This monochromatic colour scheme in tints and tones of purple relies on strong contrasts of texture and form.

Method

1 Soak your foam and position it off-centre on the dish.

2 Cut the ornamental cabbages short and insert in the foam at the rear.

3 Position the roses at various lengths so the longest spill over the rim of the dish. Add the baubles.

4 Roll the length of ribbon on its side. Take a wire and bind tightly around the ribbon towards the base. You will thus form an attractive rosette.

5 Fill in the remaining space with the *Limonium* cut into short lengths. If you keep the lengths long you will find it difficult to create a strong mass and the overall shape of the design will suffer.

Berries from the garden

The magic of this design is the contrast of the green leaves and shiny red berries with the blue of the container. This design will give winter cheer for weeks.

Design tip

Skimmia is extremely easy to grow in the garden. Make sure that you purchase a shrub that is both male and female, such as *Skimmia japonica* subsp. *reevesiana*, so that you get both flowers and berries at the same time.

Method

1 Fill the bowl half full with water.
2 Cut the stems of *Skimmia* short and mass in the bowl.
3 Change the water every other day and cut a small amount off the length of each stem and your design will last and last.

All wrapped up

You will need

- piece of floral foam
- black plastic bin liner
- length of sisal fabric to wrap round your foam
- berried ivy (*Hedera helix* 'Arborescens')
- 5-7 walnuts, gilded
- cocktail or kebab sticks
- 5-7 round flowers, such as mini *Gerbera*
- 2 roses
- 1 stem of lisianthus (*Eustoma*)

Design tip

You could add baubles or ribbon to add more sparkle. Alternatively, just lightly spray a few of the ivy leaves with gold.

This design uses sisal fabric but it could be created with any off-cut of fabric, or even a thick table napkin.

Method

1   Cut up the foam to the size required.

2   Cover the bottom and sides of the foam with black plastic bin liner.

3   Wrap the sisal around the container you have created.

4   Insert stems of berried ivy so that they create a strong structure (Techniques page 93), making sure that the stems cascade downwards over the sides of the container.

5   Insert a cocktail stick through the soft part at the base of each walnut. Position these through the design.

6   Cut the flowers short and insert into foam.

Pure colour

A sunburst of colour in this design of chilli peppers and roses.

You will need

- **low bowl**
- **floral foam**
- **15 yellow roses**
- **5-7 stems of chilli peppers (depending on how many peppers are on the stem)**
- **5 stems of *Trachelium* or sprigs of small leaved evergreen foliage such as box, myrtle or conifer**

Take care

When handling chillies be sure to wash your hands immediately afterwards and before any contact with the eyes as they are a powerful irritant and can cause great pain.

Method

1 Place a piece of soaked foam in the bowl so that the foam rises up to the rim but not above. The foam should fill most but not all of the opening so that water can be added easily. Strap in place with florists' tape.

2 Cut the roses short and place centrally to form a roughly circular pattern.

3 Remove the chillies from the main stem but ensure that they are on a secondary stem. This may be short. Create a circle of chillies around the roses.

4 Add the green *Trachelium*, or foliage cut into small neat sprigs, around the chillies, so that the foam is completely covered and angled over the rim of the container.

In the cube

This quick and easy idea brings inexpensive festive sparkle to any corner of the room.

You will need

- glass cube container – mine is 12.5 cm (5 in) square
- coloured baubles
- small block of foam
- wooden skewers
- garden twine
- cellophane
- blue spruce (*Picea pungens*)
- 4 red roses
- *Hypericum* berries, sprayed gold

Design tip

If you have a shallow dish that fits just inside the container you could use this instead.

Skimmia **berries would work well instead of the** *Hypericum* **berries.**

If your container is larger than this one simply use more roses.

Method

1 Fill the container with baubles.

2 Create a grid using the wooden skewers and the garden twine to keep the structure in place. Place it on top of the container.

3 Soak your foam and then cover the base with cellophane using florists' tape to keep it in place. This will stop the foam from dripping into the vase.

4 Place the block of foam on top of the grid and place the blue spruce to create an outline on two overlapping levels.

5 Position the four roses in the centre of the design.

6 Use the gilded *Hypericum* berries to fill the area between the spruce and the roses.

The Christmas tree

You will need

- **small Christmas tree (Abies nordmanniana)**

To decorate the pot
- **decorative paper and contrasting twine**
- **bun moss**

To decorate the tree
- **dried orange slices (Techniques page 96), studded with cloves**
- **miniature chillies, gilded Eucalyptus pods, fir cones and orchid tubes**
- **strong decorative wire**
- **1 stem spray Chrysanthemum**
- **1 stem Chinese lanterns (Physalis) - fresh or dried**

For the garland
- **Hypericum sprayed gold**
- **thin decorative wire**

For the star
- **3 medium long cinnamon sticks**
- **raffia**

This fun little tree combines natural materials and brightly coloured wire to create an alternative festive centerpiece.

Method

1 Place the bun moss at the base of the tree. Besides looking decorative this will help to retain moisture.

2 Wrap the decorative paper around the pot and secure with twine in a contrasting colour.

3 Wrap the orchid tubes with wire and fill two thirds with water. Place an individual *Chrysanthemum* head on a short stalk in each one and hang on the tree.

4   Select decorative wire of a suitable colour
    to embellish your cones and pods
    and to provide a hook for
    hanging.

5   Create a garland by
    threading
    Hypericum berries
    onto wire and
    twisting the wire
    around the
    berry to secure.
    Wind lengths of
    garland through
    the tree.

6   To make the star
    place the cinnamon
    sticks one on top of
    the other to create the
    shape. Secure with raffia.
    Tie to the tree with the raffia ends.

7   Wire the stalks of the individual Chinese
    lanterns and hook on the tree. If your Chinese
    lanterns get squashed blow air gently into the
    tiny opening at the tip to re-inflate.

Table centrepiece

A few snippets from the garden give a luxurious base to a design of dark winter anemones and vibrant orange roses.

Method

1 Create a strong structure of foliage for a rectangular container (Techniques page 93). You will still be able to see the foam but it will not be obvious.

2 Place your flowers through the design, making sure to keep within the boundaries of your foliage outline.

3 For the napkins, tie a stem of lily grass around a folded napkin and insert a sprig of *Hypericum* underneath the knot.

Design tip

Anemones are sometimes thought of as a spring flower but in fact they are available from November. They do have a soft stem so if it is difficult to insert them into the foam use a length of a harder stem (such as *Hypericum*) to first make a hole.

Chilli Christmas

This dazzling design, created with a strong background of conifer, includes cinnamon sticks, orange slices, chillies and even baby aubergines!

You will need

· **round container**
· **gold plate**
· **floral foam**
· **foliage such as blue spruce, conifer and** *Skimmia* **berries**
· **10-12 red roses such as 'Torero' or 'El Toro'**
· **Cinnamon sticks, dried orange slices, chilli peppers, poppy seed heads, baby aubergines and any other festive decorations you have to hand**

Design tip

Ripening vegetables give off ethylene gas which shortens the life of flowers. Roses are less susceptible to ethylene than many flowers but carnations are particularly vulnerable.

Method

1 Place the foam in the container so that it rises above the rim.

2 Use the spruce and other foliage to create a strong outline that is balanced from all sides (see Techniques page 93).

3 Add your roses throughout the design so that they reinforce the overall form.

4 Wire all the decorative elements (see Techniques page 95) and add them to the design.

5 Place your arrangement on the plate and top up regularly with water.

All aglow

A warm and fiery mass of garden foliage and bloom chrysanthemums.

You will need

- **a low dish – this will be obscured so it can be plastic, glass or ceramic**
- **floral foam**
- **florists' tape**
- **a thick candle to harmonise with the plant material**
- **a variety of garden foliage – I have used pine (*Pinus*), spruce (*Abies*), juniper (*Juniperus*), holly (*Ilex*) and other conifer.**
- **3 large baubles and 3 bunches of small baubles in a harmonising colour**
- **several artificial leaves**
- **thick wire or flower stems**
- **3 bloom chrysanthemums**

Design tip

I have used a few artificial gilded leaves but this design would also be effective using plain green leaves such as salal (*Gaultheria*) or Ivy (*Hedera*) lightly sprayed gold.

Method

1 Soak the foam and tape it into the container. Make sure it rises above the rim.

2 Secure the candle in the foam.

3 Create a strong base using the garden foliage, angling the stems downwards and creating a low, oval shape (Techniques page 93).

4 Wire each bauble by inserting a thick wire into the foam and placing the bauble over the top. Alternatively, you could insert a short length of stem – *Hypericum* for instance – into the opening at the top of the bauble.

5 Add the chrysanthemums and baubles in groups to complete the design.

Bittersweet

The striking red and yellow berries stay on the branch once dried so this wreath can be used again and again to give winter sunshine.

You will need

- wire frame of a size to suit
- fresh dogwood (*Cornus*)
- florists' wire
- fresh or dried sprays of bittersweet (*Celastrus*)
- piece of floral foam about 15 cm (6 in) long and 5 cm (2 in) in diameter
- coated 1.25 cm (half in) chicken wire
- 10–12 vibrant coloured roses
- kumquats and tangerines

Design tip

Chicken wire which is coated in green plastic is easier to manipulate and is less likely to slice through the foam than the galvanized wire.

Take care

All parts of the *Celastrus* are poisonous to humans if eaten so do not use if there are young children who may put the fruits in their mouths.

Method

1 Wrap lengths of dogwood around the wire frame and secure in place with lengths of wire. Use sufficient dogwood so that the wire frame is well covered.

2 Trail the stems of bittersweet through the wreath.

3 Soak the foam and wrap the chicken wire around and secure the open ends with wire to make a parcel.

4 Take a couple of lengths of florists' wire and pass under the chicken wire and onto the metal frame. Twist the wire ends together firmly to attach the foam cage securely to the wreath.

5 Wire the tangerines and kumquats (Techniques page 96).

6 Place the flowers and fruits in the foam to follow the circular movement of the wreath.

Roundabout

Unbelievably easy to make but a design that will catch the eye.

You will need

- **round plate – this could be gold, silver, copper or ceramic but you need to choose baubles to colour co-ordinate**
- **florists' fix**
- **6 baubles**
- **6 mini *Gerbera***
- **central ornament such as a minimalist Christmas tree or a thick Church candle**

Design tip

Choose baubles that have openings sufficiently large for water to be poured in easily. Using fix on the base of the baubles may remove some of the colour.

Take care

Take care when making this design with glass baubles. I squeezed one too hard and it shattered into a thousand pieces. Plastic baubles would be safer to use.

Method

1 Position the ornament or candle in the centre of the plate.

2 Remove the tops from the baubles and fill with water. Avoid spilling water over the baubles as fix will not adhere to a wet surface.

3 Take a small amount of fix and place at the base of each bauble. Position them around the plate at regular intervals.

4 Cut each mini *Gerbera* short and place one in each bauble.

Gorgeous green

You will need

- **low round dish**
- **floral foam**
- **blue spruce**
- **mixed foliage such as conifer, *Pittosporum*, box (*Buxus*), or myrtle (*Myrtus*)**
- **small/medium *Aspidistra* leaves**
- **flat or bun moss**
- **green santini chrysanthemums**
- **3-4 heads (about half a stem) green *Cymbidium* orchids**
- **decorations to add sparkle – I have used artificial glitter grapes and wax apples**
- **hairpins of medium gauge wire**
- **orchid tubes**

Design tip

***Cymbidium* stems normally have 9-14 heads. Use any left over to make the design on the front cover or on page 39.**

This glossy, glorious green design looks good enough to eat.

Method

1   Tape a block of well soaked foam in the container, so that it rises above the rim of the container.

2   Create an outline with blue spruce (Techniques page 93).

3   Manipulate 3-4 *Aspidistra* leaves (Techniques page 97) and add to the design.

4   Fill in with your mixed foliage and moss to create a dome shape. Fix the moss to the foam with hairpins of wire.

5   When complete the volume of the plant material should dominate over that of the container in the ratio of one to one and a half.

6   Place the heads of the orchids in individual tubes and add to the design.

You will need

- 3 small glass containers –
  the ones shown are
  8 cm (3 in) square
- stapler or florists' fix
- 3 *Aspidistra* leaves
- 3 pine cones
- 1 red rose
- 1 red carnation (*Dianthus*)
- spray of holly berries or
  crab apples

Design tip

**The flowers used would
all last for the length of a
dinner party without
water, but if you want
them to last any longer
then put the stems in an
orchid tube which can be
disguised with a leaf.**

One, two, three

This row of tiny cube vases would look very
special as individual place settings or positioned
in a line along the centre of a table. The front
cover shows the same design but uses heads of
Cymbidium orchids in toning colours.

Method

1 Roll the *Aspidistra* leaves and secure with a small staple or piece of
   florists' fix. Make sure the rolls are large enough to rise just above the
   rim of the vases.

2 Position the cones inside the rolled leaves and place carefully into
   the vases.

3 Cut the flowers short and place beside the leaf.

Heavenly Hippeastrum

This simple design is very striking and will last for up to ten days if the water is changed daily.

Method

1 Fill the vase with water and place the *Hippeastrum* so that their stems are vertical.

2 Push the lengths of pine down the sides of the vase to add textural interest.

You will need

· tall cylinder vase
· 10-12 amaryllis (*Hippeastrum*), in a variety of colours
· a few short lengths of pine (*Pinus*)

Design tips

The pine in the water will mean that you must change the water in this design as regularly as possible to retain freshness.

If you want to give the *Hippeastrum* extra support insert a length of cane up each stem.

A bed of orchids

You will need

- **square or rectangular low plastic container**
- **floral foam**
- **1 large stem of blue spruce**
- **1 stem of white *Cymbidium* orchid**
- **orchid tubes**
- **cranberries**
- **angel hair**

Design tip

If you cannot get hold of tubes make holes in the foam with a strong stem such as that of a rose. The orchid heads can then be inserted easily. Fresh orchids should last about 10 days.

The *Cymbidium* orchids give this otherwise traditional design a touch of luxury.

Method

1 Place the soaked foam into the container so that it rises above the rim.

2 Create a three dimensional outline using the blue spruce (Techniques page 93).

3 Cut the orchid heads off the main stem and place each one in an orchid tube filled with water.

4 Place the orchid heads through the design evenly.

5 Sprinkle the cranberries over the design.

6 Spread a little angel hair over the arrangement to add sparkle.

Ring of roses

Turn a simple tumbler into a lovely, festive container in this delightful design.

You will need

· **thick white candle**
· **floral foam**
· **florists' tape and cocktail sticks**
· **6-8 small or medium red roses**
· **white or yellow *Hypericum* berries**
· **ming fern (*Asparagus umbellatus*), Myrtle (*Myrtus*), box (*Buxus*) or other small leaved evergreen foliage**
· **gold sparkle berries or gilded *Hypericum* berries (see tip)**

To make your own container:
· **glass or plastic tumbler**
· **red sisal**
· **flat moss**
· **gold reel wire**
· **gold beads and sequins**

Method

1 This container came ready made but to make your own, place the moss around the container and secure by wrapping tightly around with the red sisal. Knot the beads and sequins onto the gold reel wire and bind the moss and sisal securely in place.

2 Place the foam into the container so that it rises above the rim. Secure the candle into the foam (Techniques page 94).

3 Cut the plant material short and arrange regularly around the candle.

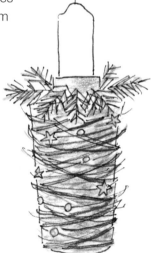

Design tip

To make your own glitter berries, dip some gilded *Hypericum* in a little glue, allow to dry for a minute and then roll in some glitter.

A touch of tartan

Tartan always brings festive cheer at Christmas and into the New Year.

You will need

· a straight sided tumbler
· double sided tape
· tartan ribbon, the same width as the height of your container
· berried ivy (*Hedera helix* 'Arborescens')
· a selection of flowers and berries such as roses, anemones and *Hypericum*

Method

1 Wrap one or two widths of double sided tape around your tumbler or plastic container.

2 Cut your ribbon to fit and wrap around the tumbler onto the tape.

3 Half fill the tumbler with water. Place several sprays of berried ivy in the water. This will create a framework.

4 Add your flowers and berries to form a rounded mass of plant material.

Design tip

This design uses a mix of flowers and berries that would be suitable for winter gleanings from the garden. Do be sure to include at least one type of flower with a round form.

Twinkling star

This star-shaped wreath uses tiny lights to make your front door stand out from the crowd.

You will need

- **5 lengths of heavy gauge wire 30 or 45 cm (12 or 18 in) long, whichever you have available**
- **stem tape**
- **3-5 stems of soft ruscus (*Danae racemosa*)**
- **reel wire**
- **battery operated fairy lights**
- **garland of artificial gold berries**

Design tip

When binding the soft ruscus to the frame, make sure that it is not so loose that the shape is obscured, but not so tight that you lose the natural movement of the foliage.

Soft ruscus can be grown easily in the garden but ensure you have both male and female plants growing close together.

Method

1 Draw a star on a large piece of paper, of the size that you would like your finished design. Measure the length of the sides.

2 Using the stem tape bind the wire together to make one long length. Use your drawing as a guide to bend the wire into a star shape and secure the ends with more stem tape.

3 Wind the soft ruscus around the wire frame and secure using reel wire.

4 Repeat this process with the gold berries and fairy lights. Bind the battery pack of the lights to the back of the wreath so that it is secure and out of the way.

5 Use a loop of reel wire to hang the star on a door handle or knocker.

Just garlands

You will need

- black plastic bags (each bag will produce over twice its length in garland)
- strong reel wire or garden twine
- medium gauge wires or cut lengths of twine
- a mass of long lasting evergreen foliage. This design uses blue spruce conifer, berried ivy (*Hedera helix* 'Arborescens'), *Skimmia japonica*, variegated holly with berries (*Ilex*) and *Elaeagnus* with a cream variegation.

Design tip

To decorate your garland with fruits, berries and cones refer to Techniques pages 95, 96.

If you wish to make a longer length of garland just knot two or three lengths of bag together.

Long, flexible garlands have been used since Roman times to decorate the home. A mixture of wonderful seasonal foliage calls for no further embellishment and is a lot easier to make than you may think.

Method

1 Condition your plant material well. Fill a large sink with water and submerge the long lasting garden foliage under water for 30-60 minutes so that it is fully charged with water.

2 Take a strong plastic black bag and with sharp scissors cut down each of the side folds to the base. Open out but leave the base intact.

3 Make bunches of foliage. These need to be kept reasonably short but quite full and bushy. Three short lengths about 12 cm (5 in) should be about right to make each bunch. Bind these together with wire or twine tightly to form one bunch. You will probably need a lot more than you think!

4 Scrunch the black bag together at one end and place the first bundle on the black bag so that the tips of the foliage extend beyond. Bind this onto the end of the bag tightly with the reel wire or twine.

5 Take a second bundle and place slightly higher up the bag, about 3-5 cm (1½-2 in), and angle it to one side. Repeat to the other side, just a little bit higher than the second bundle.

6 Create a swathe of foliage. Incorporate further swathes of other foliage as desired. You need to contrast the foliage so that fussy foliage, such as conifer, abuts another with a smoother texture such as *Skimmia* or ivy.

7 Continue in one direction down the length of the bag. You can reverse the last or last two placements so that you have two ends. It is easier than you think!

Techniques

Foam

Using floral foam

Floral foam is a water absorbing material which supports stems at virtually any angle. It is readily available at DIY stores, florists and larger supermarkets. OASIS® is a well-known brand name. Floral foam is most commonly available in a brick-sized block but is also available in cones, cylinders, rings, spheres and a myriad of other shapes. There is also a coloured foam called OASIS® Rainbow® Foam. This takes much longer to soak.

Preparing foam

Cut the piece of foam you require and place it horizontally on water that is deeper than the piece of foam you wish to soak. Allow the foam to sink under its own weight until the top is level with the water and the colour has changed from light to dark green. Always keep a reservoir of water in the bottom of your container from which the foam can draw.

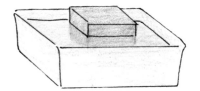

Securing foam in container

To secure foam in a dish you can either:

- Place florists' fix on the base of a four pronged disc called a 'frog'.
- Place this on the clean, dry surface of your container and impale your soaked foam on the frog.

Or:

- Use florists' tape across the top of your foam and down the two sides of the container.

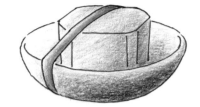

For extra security you can use both of these methods together.

Storing foam

Store unused foam that has been soaked in a tied plastic bag. In this way the foam will remain wet and keep for ages. If soaked foam is left in the open air it will dry out and will not take up further supplies of water.

Making a foliage outline

The designs on pages 6, 34, 46 and 52 are based on a strong foundation of foliage. In order to do this effectively it is recommended that:

- the foam rises higher than the container so that stems can be easily angled down then over the rim of the container. The container and arrangement appear as one, rather than as two separate parts.

- the foliage should appear to radiate from the centre of the foam. In a design where the overall appearance is round, the foliage will radiate like the spokes of a wheel if seen from above.

- for a longer design use a rectangular container with a piece of foam repeating the shape. Place a stem out of each shorter side to create the overall finished length. Radiate 2 or 3 shorter lengths out of each of the longer sides to create an overall oval form.

- For both shapes, create a strong 3 dimensional form by radiating stems from the top of the foam as well as the sides. It is essential that all stems appear to radiate from the central 'core' of the foam.

Candles

Church candles

Place four or five cocktail sticks (cut shorter if the foam is shallow) on a length of florists' tape. The tips should rise just above the tape to give security but not so that they are obvious. Wrap the tape around the candle so that the edge of the tape is on a level with the base of the candle. As an alternative to sticks you could use lengths of heavy florists' wire bent into hair pins. The effect will be the same.

Round or unusually shaped candles

Heat the ends of three heavy-gauge wires, cut down to a suitable length and ease them into the base of the candle. The heat will soften the wax and allow easy insertion.

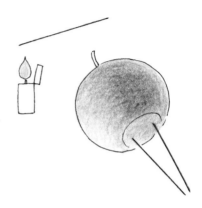

Standard tapered candles

Use specially manufactured candle holders, which are widely available. If your candle is a little wide, shave off a small amount with a warm knife. If you do not have a candle holder use the method described previously for church candles.

Bows

For a figure of eight bow, take a length of ribbon about 1 m (40 in) long. Find the central point and bring the ends over, across the centre. Take a length of medium-gauge wire and wrap it around the centre. Secondary loops can be made by having a longer length of ribbon and by making extra loops into the centre as many times as you wish.

Wiring

Wiring small cones

Take a medium-gauge wire and wrap the central point of the wire round the scales of the cone at the lowest possible point. Pull the wire tight, and then twist and take the two free ends under to the central base of the cone to create a 'stalk'.

Wiring large cones

Take two medium-gauge wires and wrap each halfway round the circumference of the scales. Twist the wires together at each side and bring them down together under the base of the cone to create a 'stalk'.

Walnuts

Walnuts have a soft spot in their base. Take a wire and simply push it through the soft spot into the centre of the nut. You could add a drop of glue for extra security, if desired.

Fruit slices

Choose fruits that have a firm flesh and few, or no, pips. Slice as thinly as possible. Place on kitchen towelling on a baking tray and cook in a slow oven (the bottom of an Aga or kitchen range or on the top of a double radiator is ideal) turning occasionally until the slices are firm. They can be varnished with a clear varnish, but this is not necessary if all the flesh is firm. To wire, take a medium-gauge wire through the slice, as close to the pith as possible, bend over and twist as close to the fruit as you can.

Fresh fruits

Take a medium or heavy gauge wire through the fruit and out the far side, about one-third of the way up the fruit. Repeat with a second wire at right-angles to the first. Bring the wires down and twist together.

Alternatively, insert wooden or plastic sticks into the fruit. The advantage of not using wires is that you can eat the fruit afterwards. Place more than one stick into a fruit to prevent rotation – two or three pieces is best.

Extending a stem

Bend a medium gauge wire so that one end is longer than the other. Place on the stem, towards the end and wrap the longer wire around the stem and the shorter end three times. The free ends should be straight and parallel to one another.

Manipulated leaves

There are many ways to manipulate leaves but the method we have used on pages 7, 33 and 78 uses an *Aspidistra* leaf which is manipulated in the following way. Fold the tip of the *Aspidistra* down to the point where the leaf meets the stalk. Angle it to one side. Take the stem and bring it backwards and over so that it can be pushed through the two layers of the folded leaf. To do this the stems needs to be reasonably long.

Glitter and spray paint

We have used special spray glue (www.fleurplus.com) but you could alternatively use spray mount or Tack 2000 from an art supplier or stationer. Spray the glue on to your flower, foliage or cone in short bursts from a distance of approximately 20 cm (8 in). Sprinkle glitter over the object into a box or onto a newspaper so that you can re-use the excess. When spraying with paint use the same procedure.

Hairpins

Hairpins are made by taking a length of wire and bending it in two. Use the gauge of wire suitable for your purpose.

Buying winter flowers

- Winter is the best time to buy orchids grown in Asia and they are often less expensive than you may think. A stem of *Cymbidium* orchid will last two to three weeks.

- Avoid buying poinsettia plants if placed outside a shop - they are vulnerable to draughts and will be short lived if they have been exposed.

- Buy amaryllis (*Hippeastrum*) in bud rather than as an open flower and they should last 10 days.

- Check that holly, *Skimmia* or other berries on foliage are plump and that none or only a few drop when very gently shaken. Spray with hairspray to prolong the life of the berries.

- *Gerbera* and germini should have a clean centre with no pollen present. The evidence of pollen means the life of the flower is near its end. The exception is a new variety of *Gerbera* called 'Gerrondo', which does not have an obvious centre.

- When purchasing *Freesia* check that colour is showing on two buds on each stem. They will not be long-lived if more than one flower is fully open on the stem.

- If buying *Anthurium* check that the tip of the spadix is not brown and the spathe has no brown blemishes.

- When purchasing lilies the length of stem up to the start of the flowers should be relatively short (about 75cm (30in)) to indicate slow strong growth. If the stem is very long the growth has been too quick and the stem will be weak.

- Do not expect a lily to open when you want it to. Lilies will stubbornly refuse to open, whatever trick you may play, until they are good and ready. I recommend buying 5 days before you want them fully open.

- Unless you are conscientious and patient do not buy *Azalea* and *Cyclamen* plants. They are wonderful but do need care and attention. I find the small headed *Cyclamen* will last much better than its larger headed relative.

- The protective petals around a rose are called 'guard' petals and can be a little distorted. These can be easily removed to give a more perfect look.

- Care should be taken when handling *Euphorbia fulgens*. The sap/milk is extremely toxic. Wash hands after working with any *Euphorbia* and keep hands away from mouth and eyes.

Caring for your flowers

- Always recut flowers and foliage immediately prior to placing in water or soaked foam. The stem ends will seal as soon as they are out of water and do not absorb water unless re-cut.

- Cut your stems at a sharp angle with clean scissors.

- Always use clean water in a clean container.

- Gerberas are particularly susceptible to bacteria so add one drop of bleach to a large vase of water.

- Do not add lemonade because although it is food for the flower it is also food for bacteria. Use special food for cut plant material and make up according to the manufacturer's instructions.

- Never hammer or bash the stems as the damaged cells encourage the growth of bacteria.

- Anemones love water so if they are looking tired submerge under water for half an hour before re-arranging.

- Amaryllis (*Hippeastrum*) have hollow stems which will curl back onto themselves once under water. You should re-cut the stem ends daily. Alternatively, tie a length of wool or wrap a rubber band around the stem close to the end.

- The stems of calla lilies (*Zantedeschia*) produce an enormous amount of bacteria. Make sure you trim a little off the end and change the water daily.

- To revive a rose that has wilted cut off at least 7 cm (3 in) from the stem end and immediately submerge the flower and stem under water for half an hour. It is not an infallible method but it usually works if the rose has not come to the end of its natural life.

Flower index

A selection of flowers available November – February

Blue and Purple

Eryngium (sea holly)

Eustoma (lisianthus) also available in pink, white, yellow and bi-coloured.

Hedera helix (berried ivy) (B)

Iris also available in white, yellow.

Red and Pink

Anthurium also available in shades of white, purple, green, variegated.

Freesia also available in shades of yellow, orange, white, purple, brown.

Gerbera also available in white, yellow, salmon, brown, orange.

Gloriosa also in yellow

Key: (F) = foliage, (B) = berries.

Limonium
(sea lavender)
also available in
pink, white.

Picea pungens
(blue spruce) (F)

Rosa 'Cool Water'

Viburnum tinus
(laurestinus) (B)

Anemone also
available in white,
red, pink.

Hippeastrum
(amaryllis) also
available in white,
variegated.

Hypericum (St. John's
wort) also available in
brown, white, green,
yellow (B).

Ilex verticillata (holly)
also available in
yellow (B).

Rosa 'Aqua'

Rosa 'Grand Prix'

Orange and Yellow

Acacia (mimosa)

Anigozanthos (kangaroo paw) also available in red, green and black/yellow

Mahonia (F) and flowers

Physalis alkekengi (Chinese lanterns) dried

White and Cream

Chamelaucium (wax flower) also available in pink

Chrysanthemum also available in red, yellow, orange, green, pink, purple.

Dendrobium (Singapore orchid) also available in pink, purple, green.

Gypsophila (baby's breath) also available in pink.

Green

Chrysanthemum 'Santini'

Cymbidium orchid also available in pink, yellow, brown, white.

Trachelium also available in white, purple.

Cupressus (cypress) also in gold (F).

Pyracantha (fire bush) (B)

Ranunculus (turban flower) also available in shades of red, pink, white, orange.

Rosa 'Cherry Brandy'

Rosa 'Gold Sphinx'

Rosa 'Milva'

Lilium (lily) also available in red, pink, orange, yellow.

Rosa 'Avalanche'

Rosa 'Vendella'

Symphoricarpos (snowberry) also available in pink

Narcissus (paperwhite)

Buxus sempervirens (box) (F)

Dianthus 'Prado' (carnation)

Rosa 'Florence Green'

Helleborus (stinking hellebore)

Brassica (ornamental cabbage) (F)

105

Glossary

Aggregates
The name given to coloured gravel or small stones, used to add texture or to hide unsightly mechanics.

Angel hair
Also known as Lametta, this is a gold, thread like substance made from metallic or plastic foil. It is also available made from fine filament glass fibre wool.

Bullion or Boullion wire
A fine decorative wire with a curl or bend to it that gives a fine shimmer to designs.

Decorative wire
Available in many different colours and thickness, this wire is used to add colour and create other decorative effects. You can buy this from many good craft shops and some garden centres.

Florists' fix
An adhesive putty that is purchased on a roll. OASIS ® Fix is a brand that is widely available.

Florists' tape
This is a strong tape that can be purchased in various widths. It will adhere to wet surfaces including soaked foam.

Frog
A green plastic disc with four prongs that comes in both large and small sizes. Ideal used in conjunction with fix to secure foam.

LED lights
Operated by a small battery, these lights are waterproof and are available in a whole spectrum of colours.

Orchid tubes

Singapore (*Dendrobium*) and *Cymbidium* orchids are supplied to florists in short plastic tubes with a rubber top with a hole for the stem. Your florist may well be happy to let you have these as they are often thrown away. They are also available from craft shops and specialist suppliers.

Picks

A pick is a single stem bearing multiple side stems of artificial plant material such as berries, flowers and fruit.

Raffia

This may be purchased in a natural tone or in a wide range of dyed colours. Raffia can be looped, made into bows or tied round containers and bunches to give a natural look.

Reel wire

So called because it comes on a reel. It is also known as binding wire. This is excellent for fastening moss onto a frame.

Sisal

Sisal is a natural material derived from *Agave sisalana* leaves. It is available in a wide range of colours and is a very useful filler.

Stem tape

This is used to disguise wires that have been added to extend or give support to fresh plant material. It also conserves water in the stem.

NB
Many of the items mentioned in the Glossary may be purchased from Hobbycraft in the UK (www.hobbycraft.co.uk) and from Michaels in the USA (www.michaels.com)

The Judith Blacklock
Flower School

The Judith Blacklock Flower School offers intensive, structured courses in all aspects of flower arranging and the business of floristry. In a quiet secluded mews in Knightsbridge, London, Judith and her team of dedicated teachers give professional information and practical learning skills, using the most beautiful flowers and foliage, that are relevant to participants from all over the world.

From basic design through to the most advanced contemporary work there is a course suitable for every level of expertise.

Private, team building and structured group lessons are available on request.

The Judith Blacklock Flower School

4/5 Kinnerton Place South, London SW1X 8EH

Tel. +44 (0)20 7235 6235

school@judithblacklock.com

www.judithblacklock.com

Acknowledgements

Photography

Scott Forrester: pages 61, 63, 87
Tom Langford: pages 1, 2, 71
Jackie Noble: page 75
Tobias Smith: pages 5, 7,11, 14, 15, 17, 19, 21, 23, 25, 26, 27, 29, 30, 31, 32, 33, 32, 35, 37, 39, 41, 43, 45, 47, 48, 49, 51, 52, 53, 55, 57, 59, 64, 65, 66, 67, 69, 73, 77, 79, 80, 81, 83, 85, 89, 90, 91

Brand X Pictures: page 6 (bottom left and bottom right)
International Flower Bulb Bureau: pages 9, 13
©iStockphoto.com/Graeme Gilmour: page 44 (bottom centre)
©iStockphoto.com/Andrew Lewis: page 104 (2nd row, 3rd from left)
©iStockphoto.com/Miroslaw Modzelewski: page 38 (bottom left)
©iStockphoto.com/Guillermo Perales Gonzalez: page 44 (bottom right)
©iStockphoto.com/Stepan Popov: page 44 (bottom left)
©iStockphoto.com/Steven van Solde: page 3
©iStockphoto.com/Marek Szumlas: page 38 (bottom right)
©iStockphoto.com/Ivan Vasilev: page 6 (bottom centre)
©PhotoDisc: pages 100, 101

Line Drawings: Tomoko Nakamoto
Botanical Editor: Dr. Christina Curtis
Assistant Editor: Rachel Petty

Thank you to David Austin roses (www.davidaustinroses.com) for supplying the roses on pages 5, 41, and 53.

Many people have helped with this book. I would like to extend a big thank you to Amanda Hawkes, my invaluable designer whose skill and expertise are a joy with which to work. Tomoko Nakamoto has created the most delicate of line drawings which are a pleasure to view. Christina Curtis has checked the botanical text with her consistent professionalism. Rachel Petty has co-ordinated photographs and text and helped with the designs. The team at the flower school have provided inspiration, ideas and moral support. I must make special mention of Chika Yoshida, Takako Yodoi, Ranna Sayama and a very special teacher at the school, Dawn Jennings. I must also mention Gail Bearman, Pat King, Sue Stevenson and Rachel Temple for their help and expertise. Tobias Smith is a photographer with a great future – he is patient, quick thinking and understands flowers. I would like to thank him for his dedicated work in providing most of the photographs in this book – toby_smith@talk21.com.